SABI HILMI

ARCHANGEL RAPHAEL'S HEALING TOUCH

A Child's Story of Wellness & Calm

Contents

Prologue

Welcome to my series of Archangel Books for Children, where young readers are introduced to the powerful, loving and spiritual presence of the Archangels, each guiding them through different areas of their lives. This series is thoughtfully crafted to help children understand how the Archangels provide support, protection, and wisdom in their everyday experiences, be it emotional, mental, or physical well-being. Each book in this series focuses on a different Archangel, showing how these celestial beings assist children in navigating their feelings, building self-confidence, and overcoming challenges.

Through engaging stories and relatable situations, my series of Archangel Books also introduces children to the idea of a higher power that is always available to them, offering comfort and guidance. These books are designed not only to entertain but also to empower children, helping them develop a strong sense of self and a deeper awareness of the spiritual support surrounding them.

It is my hope that this series will inspire children to feel safe, loved, and confident as they grow, knowing that they are never alone on their journey through life.

With Angelic Love & Light,

Sabi Hilmi, Author

Introduction

Welcome to "Archangel Raphael's Healing Light," a special adventure for young readers to understand Wellness and Calm!

In this story, you'll meet Archangel Raphael, a magical angel who is always ready to heal any problem or discomfort. He will take you on a journey where he helps a young child discover the magical healing light that is available to everyone.

Through fun stories and simple lessons, Archangel Raphael will teach you how to manage your emotions, practice self-care, and find harmony, especially when feelings of anxiety arise. This book provides soothing and practical steps for emotional and physical well-being.

May the bright green light of Archangel Raphael guide you, leading you to a deeper understanding of wellness and how to stay calm.

Get ready to join Archangel Raphael as he shares his special secrets with you!

Chapter 1: Archangel Raphael the Healer

Archangel Raphael guides children to understand the power of healing, helping them face life's challenges while staying calm and centred. Through his teachings, children learn to embrace good health, comfort, and harmony, allowing them to handle difficulties with hope and faith. Archangel Raphael encourages emotional, mental and physical well-being.

A young boy named Rafee sat on his bed, holding his stomach tightly as a dull ache bothered him. He had been feeling anxious for days, and now the worry had started to make his body hurt. He was nervous about an upcoming sports event at school, and the fear of letting his team down kept going through his mind. His stomach felt like it was in knots, and there was a tightness in his chest that wouldn't go away.

Just as Rafee's frustration grew, a soft green glow appeared in the room, bringing with it a warm, peaceful feeling. "Hello, Rafee," said a voice full of kindness. "I am Archangel Raphael, the angel of healing. I've come to help you with both your worries and the discomfort in your body."

"How can you help me and what does healing mean?" Rafee asked, curious and hopeful. Archangel Raphael knelt beside him and placed a comforting hand on his shoulder. "Healing means to return something back to good health. Can you see that the word heal is within the word health?! I can show you how to heal both your mind and your body. Sometimes, when we feel anxious or scared, it can make our bodies hurt too. But together, we can ease that pain."

Rafee looked down at his aching stomach, still unsure. "But what if it doesn't go away?" he asked softly. Archangel Raphael smiled warmly and said "Healing might take some time, Rafee. But with patience, trust, and belief, your body knows how to heal itself. You're not alone in this journey, and together, we'll ease the pain. Now, let's try by closing your eyes and imagine my green light filling you from head to toe, slowly releasing all the thoughts from your mind. You can also put your hands out in front of you with your palms facing up to let the green light flow through your hands and into certain points of your body. Today, let's try one hand on your chest and the other on your tummy as this is where you feel the discomfort."

Rafee followed these instructions and shortly after, the pain in his chest and stomach faded away so magically. His racing thoughts about the sports event started to calm down.

"Remember, Rafee," Archangel Raphael said softly, "when you feel anxious, your body feels it too and creates symptoms of discomfort. Our feelings and our bodies are connected in a special way, so by calming your mind, you can help your body feel better. You have the power to bring calm and wellness to yourself whenever you need it."

Rafee smiled, feeling lighter and more at ease. The ache in his stomach was gone, and he no longer felt as worried about the sports event.

Chapter 2: Discover Calmness with Breathwork

Archangel Raphael guided Rafee to sit comfortably in the garden, surrounded by beautiful flowers, green grass, large trees and sounds of birds singing. "One of the ways we can find calm is through some magical breathwork, especially whilst connecting with nature," he said with a gentle smile. "Ready to try?"

Rafee nodded with excitement. "Let's start with a breathing technique called box breathing." "It helps to calm the mind and bring balance to your body. It's called box breathing because, as you go through each step, you can imagine you're drawing the shape of a box in your mind!"

Now, step 1 - breathe in for three silent counts in your head (1-2-3), step 2 - hold your breath for three counts (1-2-3), step 3 - breathe out for three counts (1-2-3), and step 4 - hold your breath for three counts (1-2-3)."

Rafee followed Archangel Raphael's instructions, and quickly felt his body relaxing with the tension melting away. "Good job, Rafee," Archangel Raphael praised, with a warm smile. "Whenever you feel overwhelmed or anxious, using box breathing can help you find calm and balance, and you'll see that your thoughts may even disappear!"

"Let's make this experience even more magical, when we sit or walk barefoot on the ground, we're practising something called 'grounding.' This means we're absorbing the earth's powerful energy through our feet, which also helps heal and balance our body. Archangel Raphael gently guided Rafee to a nearby tree. "Sometimes, when you feel lightheaded or unsteady, hugging a tree can help you feel more connected and balanced." Archangel Raphael said gently." Rafee wrapped his arms around a large tree, feeling its solid, powerful energy flowing through him.

"Now that you're connected to the ground, let's work on your breathing again. Out here in nature, you can breathe in the fresh air and let it fill your lungs with even more calming energy."

Archangel Raphael then pointed to the bright sun shining above them. "Look at the sunlight, Rafee, it's warm and full of life. Did you know that the sun gives you Vitamin D and that makes you feel happier? Feel the sun's warmth on your skin, the solid ground beneath your feet, and the cool breeze around you. Nature has a way of helping us heal when we connect with it. The more you practise this, the easier it will be to find your calm whenever you need it."

Rafee opened his eyes slowly, feeling lighter and more relaxed. He looked up at the tree and then at the sun, appreciating the natural world around him. "I feel so much better, thank you!" he said softly, a smile spreading across his face.

"That's wonderful, Rafee," Archangel Raphael said warmly. "Remember, the earth and the sun are always there to help you ground yourself. Whenever you feel stressed just come outside, breathe in the fresh air, feel the sun's warmth, and connect with the world around you."

Chapter 3: Understanding Your Emotions

A rchangel Raphael sat next to Rafee and showed him a bright, colourful chart. "Each of these colours stands for a different feeling; blue means sadness, red is for anger, yellow shows happiness, and green is for calm." He explained. Rafee looked at the chart, fascinated by how different colours could represent the feelings inside him.

Archangel Raphael said. "Let's start by working out how you feel right now. Which colour best matches your emotion at the moment?" Rafee studied the chart and pointed to blue "I feel a bit sad." Archangel Raphael replied "Sadness is natural and it's okay to feel it. Now, think about a time you felt happy. Which colour would you choose?"

Rafee's face lit up as he pointed to yellow. "When I play with my dog, I feel really happy." "Great, animals are very special and they have an amazing way of cheering us up quickly!" Archangel Raphael said. "Even though your dog isn't here with you right now, just by thinking about him, you can change your emotion from sad to happy - how clever is that? Never forget that emotions usually are created by our thoughts, so we have to keep our mind as positive as possible."

They continued discussing different situations, using the chart to explore Rafee's feelings. With each example, Rafee became more comfortable expressing his emotions and understanding their causes. Archangel Raphael's presence made the process feel safe and supportive.

"Remember, Rafee, understanding your feelings is the first step to handling them," Archangel Raphael said, gently resting a hand on Rafee's shoulder. "It's okay to feel different emotions throughout the day, and by understanding them, you gain the power to get through them or change them." Rafee smiled, feeling a sense of relief. With Archangel Raphael's guidance and the colourful chart as a tool, he felt more confident, knowing he could handle his emotions quickly and find balance within himself.

Archangel Raphael smiled gently. "Feelings can be strong, but they don't have to control you. Think of your emotions like waves in the ocean. Sometimes they're big, sometimes they're small, but they always come and go. And with this chart and your breathwork, you can ride those waves instead of letting them knock you down."

Rafee looked at the chart again, feeling a sense of control he hadn't felt before. "So, even if I'm really angry or scared, I can figure out why and start to feel calm again?"

"Exactly," Archangel Raphael said kindly. "You don't need to fight or hide those feelings. Just notice them, take a deep breath, and they will begin to soften especially if you use the green light in your imagination. The more you understand your emotions, the stronger and calmer you'll become. I'm always here for you, Rafee, and so is your own inner strength."

Rafee felt comforted by Archangel Raphael's words, realising that he had the power to manage his feelings and find calm whenever he needed it.

Chapter 4: Magical Tapping for Stress Relief

I t was a busy day at home for Rafee and his family. Rafee decided to sit quietly in one of the empty rooms, as he felt a bit stressed by all the noise and activity. Sensing Rafee's discomfort, Archangel Raphael appeared beside him.

"Today, I'll teach you how to use gentle tapping on your body to relieve stress," Archangel Raphael said, with a very comforting voice. Rafee looked up and asked "What is tapping and how does it help?"

"Tapping is an easy way to help you feel better when you feel stressed. Stress happens when too many worries or emotions build up within you, so gently tapping on your body helps to release them and make both your mind and body feel relaxed."Archangel Raphael explained.

Rafee was excited to learn and try this technique. Archangel Raphael used a soft cushion to show Rafee an example of the technique. "Using your fingers on one hand, start tapping gently on and around your collarbone. Feel the rhythm of the taps and notice how it brings a sense of relaxation."

Rafee copied the movement, his fingers softly tapping against his collarbone. As he continued, he felt a strange but pleasant sensation, like a wave of calmness spreading through his body. "This is strange but it works!" Rafee said, smiling.

"Yes! Now try tapping just above your eyebrows on your forehead. Archangel Raphael encouraged. This area holds a lot of tension when you are stressed."

Rafee moved his fingers up to his forehead, following the gentle tapping rhythm. With each tap, his mind seemed to let go of the thoughts that had been swirling around. "It's like my head is clearing out my stressful thoughts," he whispered, surprised at how quickly he felt better.

"Exactly," Archangel Raphael said. "Tapping helps release all the tightness you hold on to throughout the day. Now, let's tap the sides of your ribs, just below your armpits. This is another area where stress can hide."

With each tap, Rafee felt lighter, as if a weight had been lifted from his small shoulders. "Remember, Rafee," Archangel Raphael continued, "these techniques are tools you can use whenever you feel stressed. When your body is relaxed, your mind can find its calm centre more easily, and happier emotions will then grow in your heart."

Archangel Raphael smiled down at him. "Whenever you feel stress or worry creeping in, just remember tapping will make you feel calm and that there's nothing to be stressed about."

Rafee was grateful for Archangel Raphael's guidance and the new skills he had learned. With these magical tapping techniques, Rafee knew he had a special way to find relief from stress anytime he needed it.

Chapter 5: Taking Care of your Body

Archangel Raphael teaches Rafee the importance of a healthy diet, exercise, and sleep. They make a plan together to include these wellness practices in Rafee's daily routine.

One morning, Archangel Raphael met Rafee in the kitchen. "Today, we'll talk about taking care of your body," Archangel Raphael said with a gentle smile. "A healthy diet, regular exercise, and good sleep are important for your overall well-being."

Rafee listened carefully as Archangel Raphael explained, "Eating a variety of fruits, vegetables, whole grains, and lean proteins gives your body the nutrients it needs. Let's start by making a colourful salad together."

They chopped vegetables and mixed them into a vibrant salad. "See how many colours we have here? Each colour represents different nutrients that help keep you healthy," Archangel Raphael explained. Can you see that most vegetables are the colour green? Just like my healing light! You can always remember my green light when you see or eat green food.

After enjoying their healthy meal, Archangel Raphael suggested, "Let's go outside for some exercise. Physical activity is great for your body and mind. Even a daily simple brisk walk, which means walking quickly, can make a big positive difference to your life. It can clear your mind and get your heart pumping nicely to make it stronger, and give you a long healthy life!" Archangel Raphael said.

Later, once they got back home, Archangel Raphael discussed the importance of sleep. "Rafee, getting enough sleep is like giving your body and mind a special gift every night," he said with a warm smile. "When you sleep, your body gets a chance to rest, recover, and grow. It's how your muscles get stronger, how your brain gets sharper, and how your heart stays healthy."

Rafee listened closely as Archangel Raphael continued, "Having a regular sleep pattern is really important too. If you go to bed and wake up at the same time each day, your body knows when it's time to wind down and get ready for sleep. It's like setting a routine that helps you feel rested and full of energy the next day."

"Your sleeping space is also important," Archangel Raphael added. "It should be clean, cosy, and calm. You can make it special by adding your favourite cuddly toys. Rafee nodded, thinking about his own room. "Does sleep really help me when I'm feeling tired?" "Absolutely," Archangel Raphael replied. "When you get enough sleep, your mood improves, your mind becomes clearer, and you'll find it easier to focus and learn new things. So, whenever you're feeling grumpy or have a hard day, good sleep can help you feel better and stronger the next morning."

Archangel Raphael smiled and added, "And remember, it's okay to take things one step at a time. Little changes can make a big difference. Keep up with your new habits, and you'll feel even better. You have everything you need to be healthy and happy. Taking care of your body helps you feel more energetic and better overall," Archangel Raphael said warmly. "Remember, I'm here to support you on your journey to wellness."

Chapter 6: Mindfulness Techniques to Relax

O ne rainy afternoon, Rafee was feeling bored and wanted to do something nice in a different part of the house. He thought of going up to the loft, a place he didn't usually spend much time in. With soft light coming in through a small window, and the sound of the rain gently tapping on the roof, there was a sense of peace that filled the space.

"This could be the perfect place to create your 'comfy corner,'" Archangel Raphael said with a warm smile. Rafee looked around and nodded. The loft felt just right for a special corner where he could relax and unwind. Together, they found a nice spot near the window, and placed a large fluffy beanbag, added soft cushions plus a thick, warm blanket. Rafee brought up a few of his favourite books and some little fidget toys that made him feel happy and calm. He also made himself a delicious hot chocolate to drink later.

"Now that your comfy corner is ready, let's sit here and practise some mindfulness techniques. Mindfulness is a way of paying close attention to what's happening right now, in the present moment. It helps you stop being sad about the past, and also stops you being worried about the future. It's like using all your senses; seeing, hearing, touch and even tasting, to notice what's around you and how you are feeling. Archangel Raphael said kindly.

"Close your eyes and listen to the sound of the rain, picture the rain washing away your worries, clearing your mind." Rafee closed his eyes, focusing on the gentle tap of raindrops against the window, imagining each sparkling drop flowing over him, helping him relax even more.

Next, Archangel Raphael handed Rafee a small, pretty journal, like a diary. "Writing in this journal can help you sort through your feelings.

It doesn't matter what you write or how many times, just let whatever is in your mind flow onto the pages." Rafee opened the journal and began to write how he felt earlier in the day and how he would like to feel instead.

Then Archangel Raphael took out a harp, the angels' favourite instrument! He began to play soft, gentle music. Rafee closed his eyes, listening to the calming melodies he felt the tension in his body and mind begin to melt away, replaced by a deep sense of relaxation.

Next, Archangel Raphael handed Rafee a set of coloured pencils and a sketchbook. "Sometimes, drawing can help you express your emotions and bring you into the present moment. Do you remember your colour chart? You can also use the coloured pencils that best describe how you are feeling. Rafee began to draw, letting his imagination flow onto the paper. As his picture came to life, he noticed how quickly his anxious thoughts drifted far away. He loved his picture!

"Ready for your hot chocolate?" Archangel Raphael asked with a smile. Rafee nodded with excitement. "Take a deep breath and enjoy the delicious smell. Now, hold the cup and feel its warmth, like a cosy blanket," Archangel Raphael said. Rafee smiled, feeling so comforted by all that he sensed so far! "Take a slow sip and notice the taste," Archangel Raphael added. Rafee sipped, letting the warm chocolate fill him with calm. He smiled, realising how even a simple cup of hot chocolate could make him feel so content. "Thank you very much for teaching me all these activities, I really can't wait to visit my cosy corner again whenever I need to relax and be mindful." Rafee said.

Chapter 7: Gentle Stretching for Flexibility

After a long day of sitting and thinking at school, Rafee started to feel a bit stiff in his body, especially his shoulders and back. Noticing this, Archangel Raphael suggested, "How about we do some gentle stretching to help your body feel better?"

Rafee looked up, curious. "Why stretching? How does that help?" he asked. "Stretching helps your body relax and lets go of any tightness that makes you feel uncomfortable. " Archangel Raphael explained. "It's like giving your muscles a little hug and waking them up."

Rafee smiled, excited to try. "Let's start by reaching up toward the ceiling, stretching your arms as high as you can," Archangel Raphael said. Rafee stretched tall, feeling his whole body lengthen. "Now, slowly lower your arms and notice how good it feels, like your body is waking up."

They continued with different stretches; twisting from side to side, reaching down to touch their toes, and rolling their shoulders back and forth. Rafee could feel the tightness in his muscles loosening with each movement, like the stiffness was being replaced by a gentle, comforting energy.

"Stretching also helps you be more mindful of how your body feels," Archangel Raphael continued. "It helps you slow down and pay attention to each part of your body, noticing where you feel tight or relaxed."

As they stretched, Archangel Raphael encouraged Rafee to take deep breaths, matching his movements to his breath. "Breathe in as you reach up, and breathe out as you relax your arms back down," Archangel Raphael guided. Rafee followed, noticing how the deep breaths really helped the stretches feel better each time.

"Stretching is a simple way to take care of your body, and when you pair it with deep breathing, it helps your mind relax too. Whenever you feel tense or tired, a few gentle stretches can help you feel refreshed."

After finishing their stretches, Rafee felt lighter and more comfortable. "Wow, I didn't know stretching could feel so good!" he said, smiling.

"Your body loves to move! And when your body feels good, your mind feels better too." Archangel Raphael said kindly.

Rafee nodded, feeling grateful for this new tool to help him relax. With Archangel Raphael's guidance, he now knew that mindful stretching was a simple yet powerful way to bring calm and comfort to both his body and mind.

Chapter 8: Archangel Raphael's Healing Stone

I n their final session together, Archangel Raphael gave Rafee a small, smooth stone. The stone shimmered softly, it was so beautiful to look at and to feel. "This stone is very special," Archangel Raphael said with a gentle smile, "This stone holds special healing energy. When you hold it, it sends soothing energy through your hands and into your entire body, especially to any areas where you might feel discomfort."

Rafee looked at the stone and held it in his hand feeling the gentle warmth that seemed to grow stronger as he held it. "As you hold this stone," Archangel Raphael continued, "let it remind you of the calming techniques we practised."

Rafee closed his eyes for a moment and thought about all the techniques he had learned to feel better. He remembered the calming breath he took when he felt anxious, the gentle touch that helped him relax, and the soothing walks in nature that cleared his mind. He thought about his cosy corner where he could sit quietly, and the joy of stretching to keep his body loose and relaxed. Each of these special memories gave him a sense of calm, knowing that he could take care of himself when emotions felt too big.

"Carry this stone everywhere with you! Whenever you feel stressed or uncomfortable, hold it close. Its healing energy will help you find calm and remind you of everything you've learned. It's like having a little piece of our time together always with you. If one day you lose it, don't worry, it will help whoever finds it in a special way for them to feel better! It's good to be generous and share healing with others, so you can even give it away as a gift. You can turn any new stone into your magical healing stone!" Archangel Raphael advised softly.

Rafee felt a deep sense of gratitude as he took the stone and carefully tucked it into his pocket. It was not just a gift, but a symbol of his journey and growth. The stone in his pocket was a comforting reminder that he carried with him not only the lessons learned but also the ability to heal any unwanted situation that may come his way.

As they stood together in the soft light of the room, Rafee looked up at Archangel Raphael, his heart full of appreciation. "Thank you for everything," Rafee said quietly. "I'll always remember what you've taught me."

Archangel Raphael's smile was full of warmth and love. "You're very welcome, Rafee," he replied. "And remember, even though you can't see me, I'm always here! Trust in yourself, and know that you have very magical healing powers to overcome any of life's challenges."

Meditation with Archangel Raphael

1. Ask someone to read these instructions for you.
2. Find a comfortable place to either lie down or sit cross-legged and close your eyes.
3. Take a few deep breaths, in through your nose and out through your mouth.
4. Imagine yourself standing in a beautiful forest, surrounded by large green trees. Feel the breeze of the air and the earth beneath your feet.
5. Imagine a bright green light as you feel a wave of calmness and relaxation
6. Archangel Raphael appears beside you, ready to bring you magical healing light.
7. Now, imagine yourself surrounded by a bright, green light. As he gently touches your shoulders, this light starts to heal any tension or discomfort you feel.
8. Repeat to yourself: "I am healed. I am whole. I am filled with Archangel Raphael's healing energy."
9. Feel these words empowering you with inner and outer wellness.
10. Take a few moments to bathe in the warmth of Archangel Raphael's light, trusting that you are always taken care of.
11. When you are ready, gently bring your awareness back to the present moment. Wiggle your fingers and toes, take a deep breath, and slowly breathe out
12. Open your eyes, feeling refreshed and completely relaxed by Archangel Raphael's presence.
13. Take a moment to express gratitude for Archangel Raphael's Healing Touch. Know that Archangel Raphael is always with you, offering his healing and calmness whenever you need it.

Archangel Raphael's Healing Qualities

Archangel Raphael is like a magician who is great at transforming negativity into positivity helping us to be well. He makes us feel comfortable and balanced, so we can handle tough situations with faith. When Archangel Raphael is around, it's like having a Healing Touch that soothes physical pain, emotional hurt, and helps us grow stronger in every way.

Physical Problem: Sometimes we experience physical pain or injuries that require healing and repairing within our body.

Emotional Problem: We might carry emotional traumas or grief from the past that stop us from creating a happier life.

Psychological Problem: We may face mental health issues such as anxiety, which can stop **us** from enjoying the present moment.

Solution: Whenever you're feeling in need of support or comfort, you can call upon Archangel Raphael for help. Imagine him wrapping you in magical light with his Healing Touch. This light helps you stay calm, balanced, and well.

Gemstone: Green Aventurine is associated with healing, harmony, and renewal, making it a suitable gemstone for connecting with Archangel Raphael's energy of healing and wellness in both physical and emotional aspects.

Conclusion

As our journey with Archangel Raphael comes to an end, we reflect on the powerful lessons of healing, wellness, and mindfulness techniques that he has shared with us. Through his Healing Touch, we've learned how to stay calm in times of difficulty and restore balance to our mind, body, and heart. Archangel Raphael's teachings have shown us how to use various techniques that are available to us, such as deep breathing and connecting to nature for extra support. As we move forward, let's carry these lessons with us, remembering that Archangel Raphael's loving presence remains with us at all times.

Remember to continue exploring the Archangel Books series, where you'll meet Archangels like Gabriel, Uriel, and Chamuel, each offering unique guidance and support in different areas of your life. Whether it's learning to express yourself confidently, healing from a tough experience, there's an Archangel ready to help you every step of the way.

Stay tuned for our upcoming range of Archangel products, including mindful colouring books, audio meditations, and much more!

Angelic Blessings,

Sabi Hilmi, Author

Website: www.sabihilmi.com/archangel-books

About the Author

Sabi Hilmi is a devoted spiritual author, practitioner, and teacher passionate about empowering both children and women through her uplifting books and transformative practices. With a profound connection to the angelic realm and an unwavering belief in the power of higher guidance, she is a renowned Angelic Healer with clients worldwide. Since becoming a mother to her son Rafael in 2020, Sabi's inspiration has deepened, driving her to create books that nurture emotional, mental, and spiritual well-being. Through her Archangel book series she spreads light, love and inner peace to all.

You can connect with me on:

🌐 https://sabihilmi.com

Also by Sabi Hilmi

Archangel Books for Children

ARCHANGEL MICHAEL'S MIGHTY SHIELD
A CHILD'S STORY OF COURAGE & PROTECTION

Empower Your Child with the Courage and Protection of Archangel Michael!

Printed in Dunstable, United Kingdom

71645386R10030